DISCOVER

The United States Government

by Barbara Brannon

Table of Contents

# Introduction

The **United States** has a **government**. The United States government has three parts. The United States government has three branches.

The Three Branches of Government

Executive Branch

Judicial Branch

The power stays balanced among the three branches. The power stays balanced among the three branches. The power stays balanced among the three branches. The power stays balanced among the three branches. The power stays balanced among the three branches. The power stays balanced among the three branches.

Legislative Branch

Words to Know

executive branch

government

judicial branch

legislative branch

president

United States

See the Glossary on page 22.

3

What Is the Legislative Branch?

The United States government has a **legislative branch**.

The Three Branches of Government

The power stays balanced among the three branches. The power stays balanced among the three branches. The power stays balanced among the three branches. The power stays balanced among the three branches. The power stays balanced among the three branches. The power stays balanced among the three branches. The power stays balanced among the three branches. The power stays balanced among the three branches. The power stays balanced among the three branches. The power stays balanced among the three branches. The power stays balanced among the three branches. The power stays balanced among the three branches. The power stays balanced among the three branches. The power stays balanced among the three branches.

Legislative Branch

Executive Branch

Judicial Branch

 The legislative branch meets in the Capitol. The United States Capitol Building is in Washington, D.C.

Chapter 1

The legislative branch has a Congress.

▲ The Congress makes laws.

The Congress has two parts.

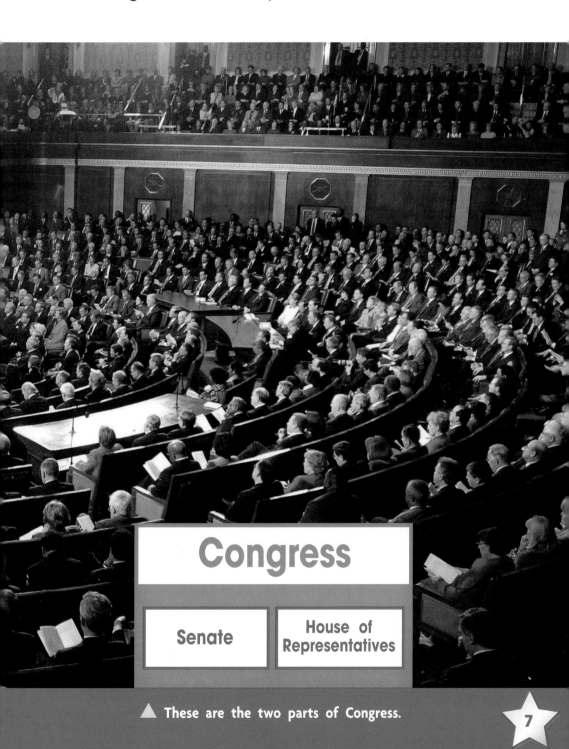

Congress

Senate | **House of Representatives**

▲ These are the two parts of Congress.

The Congress has a Senate.

▲ Each state has two senators.

SOLVE THIS

How many senators are in the Senate?

Answer: 100

The Congress has a House of Representatives.

IT'S A FACT

The House of Representatives has 435 members.

▼ There are representatives from every state.

9

What Is the Judicial Branch?

The United States government has a **judicial branch**.

The Three Branches of Government

Legislative Branch

The power stays balanced among the three branches. The power stays balanced among the three branches. The power stays balanced among the three branches. The power stays balanced among the three branches. The power stays balanced among the three branches. The power stays balanced among the three branches.

Executive Branch

Judicial Branch

The judicial branch solves problems with the laws.

The judicial branch has a Supreme Court.

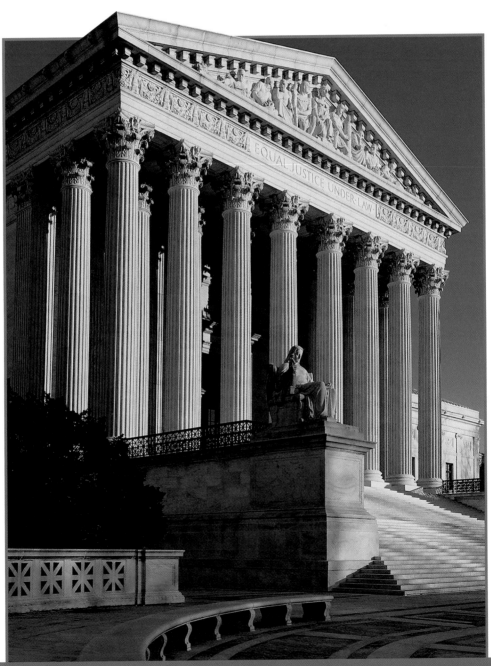

The Supreme Court is the most important court in the United States.

The Supreme Court has justices.

▲ This man was a new justice in 2005.

▲ The 2004 Supreme Court had these nine justices.

What Is the Executive Branch?

The Three Branches of Government

The power stays balanced among the three branches. The power stays balanced among the three branches. The power stays balanced among the three branches. The power stays balanced among the three branches. The power stays balanced among the three branches. The power stays balanced among the three branches. The power stays balanced among the three branches. The power stays balanced among the three branches.

Legislative Branch

Judicial Branch

Executive Branch

▲ The executive branch helps make laws.

The United States government has a leader. The **executive branch** has a **president**.

 The head of the executive branch is the president.

▲ The president lives and works in the White House.

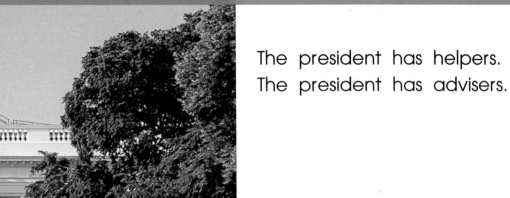

The president has helpers.
The president has advisers.

▲ Advisers help the president make important decisions.

The United States government has three branches.

The United States government has a legislative branch.

The United States government has a judicial branch.

The United States government has an executive branch.

The United States government has three branches.

legislative branch

makes laws

United States Government

judicial branch

solves problems with laws

executive branch

helps make laws

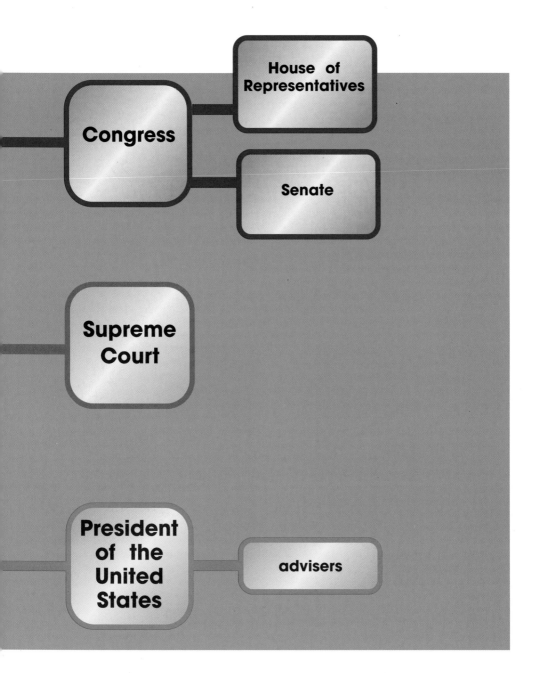

Congress

House of Representatives

Senate

Supreme Court

President of the United States

advisers

executive branch the part of government that helps make laws

The United States government has an executive branch.

government the people who are in charge of laws

The United States government has three parts.

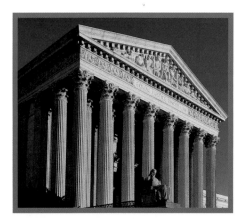

judicial branch the part of government that solves problems with laws

The United States government has a judicial branch.

legislative branch the part of government that makes laws

The United States government has a legislative branch.

president the leader of the executive branch of government

*The **president** helps make laws.*

United States a country in North America

*The **United States** has a government.*